SPACE JUMP

Contents

Written by Matt Ralphs

Collins

Felix dreams of flying

When Felix Baumgartner was a boy, he dreamt of being a skydiver. He now holds the world record for the highest skydive. This is the story of his record-breaking adventure.

Felix was born in Austria in 1969. He was interested in flying from a young age and wondered what it would be like to jump safely from great heights.

Felix Baumgartner

At the age of 16, Felix did his first skydive. Skydiving involves jumping out of an aeroplane. At first, a skydiver **free falls** and then uses a parachute to slow down for a safe landing. When he did a skydive, Felix could see the world like he never had before, from a new angle, spread out below him.

Felix liked motocross racing and worked as a motorcycle mechanic. But in his free time he did skydives at skydiving events. Felix spent as much time as he could in the sky. He wanted to see how high and how fast he could go.

Felix learns to fly

Felix joined the Austrian army. He became part of the **special forces** skydiving display team that **promoted** the army, performing at air shows. He learnt new skills, including how to parachute on to small target zones on the ground. This training came in very useful for his later adventures.

Austrian special forces skydiving

BASE jumping

After Felix left the army, he wanted other challenges. He realised that he could use his skydiving skills to try another kind of exciting parachute sport: BASE jumping.

BASE jumping is an extreme sport that developed from skydiving in the 1970s. In skydiving, the jumper leaps from a moving plane, free falls and then uses a parachute. A BASE jumper leaps from a fixed object such as a building, free falls and then opens a parachute to slow down for landing.

BASE jumpers jump from both high and low structures. While jumping from a high object can be frightening because there is a long way to drop, jumping from a low height can be even more dangerous because there is less time to open the parachute for a safe landing.

BASE jumpers jump from four different types of object. The objects are:

Buildings
usually city skyscrapers

Antennas
radio towers or masts

They often have to land in small areas, like city streets. It takes a lot of courage, skill and training.

Spans
bridges

Earth
usually off the edge of cliffs

Felix the record breaker

Felix has broken many records and jumped from some of the highest buildings in the world. In 1999, he became the world record holder for the highest BASE jump from a building.

Felix's Petronas Towers BASE jump
Location: Malaysia, Height: 451 metres
(the same height as 45 double-decker buses stacked end to end on top of each other)
Time in free fall: seven to eight seconds

In 2007, the Taipei 101 was the tallest building in the world, with 91 floors. When Felix became the first person to BASE jump from it, he broke his own world record.

Felix's Taipei 101 skydive
Location: Taiwan, Height: 509 metres
(the same height as 51 double-decker buses stacked end to end on top of each other)
Time in free fall: five seconds

9

As well as holding the record
for the highest BASE jump
from a building, Felix
wanted the record for
the lowest. In 1999, he leapt
from the arm of the Christ
the Redeemer statue in Brazil –
just 29 metres from the ground,
roughly the same as three
double-decker buses stacked
end to end on top of each other.

Felix wanted to try something never done before, so in 2003 he skydived all the way across the English Channel. This was different from any other skydive he'd done before, because he had to glide 36 kilometres during the free fall to get across the Channel.

To do the skydive, he wore a specially designed set of wings that allowed him to glide – he became a human aeroplane.

Felix's English Channel skydive
Location: English Channel, Height: 9.8 kilometres
Distance travelled: 36 kilometres
Top speed: 360 kilometres per hour
Journey duration: six minutes, 22 seconds

In BASE jumping, sometimes the focus is on what the jumper is jumping into. In 2007, Felix BASE jumped into one of the largest caves in the world. The Majlis al Jinn cave in the Sultanate of Oman is a huge hole in the ground, 121 metres deep – the height of 12 double-decker buses stacked end to end on top of each other. It is very hard to land in because it's dark and narrow.

Felix was soon looking for his next daring challenge. A man called Colonel Joe Kittinger, who had set the record for the highest skydive, gave him inspiration.

Colonel Joe Kittinger set the record when he jumped from a height of 31 kilometres in 1960. That was 21.2 kilometres higher than Felix's highest ever jump. He'd done it as part of his job, to help the United States air force learn more about what happened if a pilot had to jump out of a damaged plane.

Felix wanted to break Colonel Joe Kittinger's record. But he wanted Joe's help, because Joe understood what it was like to jump from such a height. Joe agreed and they began work on the project with an expert team.

Joe's world record skydive

Height: 31 kilometres
(the same height as 310
double-decker buses stacked end
to end on top of each other)

Time in free fall: four minutes, 36 seconds

Top speed: 988 kilometres per hour

13

Felix didn't just want to break world records. His team of
scientists, designers, engineers and medical experts wanted to
learn from the jump to help their research. They were interested
in how being high above the earth, and travelling at great speeds,
affects the human body.

The earth is surrounded by different layers of **atmosphere**. The higher you go, the less air there is to breathe. Felix wanted to jump from a height of 39 kilometres above the earth – eight kilometres higher than Joe's skydive. He would be on the very edge of space.

The environment at about 39 kilometres above Earth is called the stratosphere. It is a very dangerous place. The temperature can be low enough to freeze a person to death.

Without protection, Felix would be dead in seconds.

Felix knew that from 39 kilometres, he would be able to fall faster than ever before. This is because the atmosphere that high up is so thin, it doesn't slow falling objects down as much when they're closer to the ground.

Because of this, he hoped to travel faster than the speed of sound.

Felix's top speed compared to fast-moving vehicles

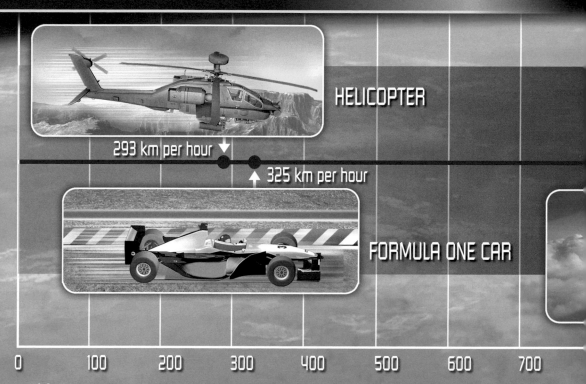

HELICOPTER

293 km per hour ▼

▲ 325 km per hour

FORMULA ONE CAR

0   100   200   300   400   500   600   700

No one knew exactly how travelling at this speed would affect the human body. Doctors were concerned that Felix's brain or other vital organs could be damaged.

He would have to use all his skills and courage to keep control of his fall. If he lost control, it would be likely he would go into a fast spin. It could make him dizzy enough to lose **consciousness** and then he wouldn't be able to open his parachute.

Felix's team created special systems like an automatic parachute opener to protect him from these dangers.

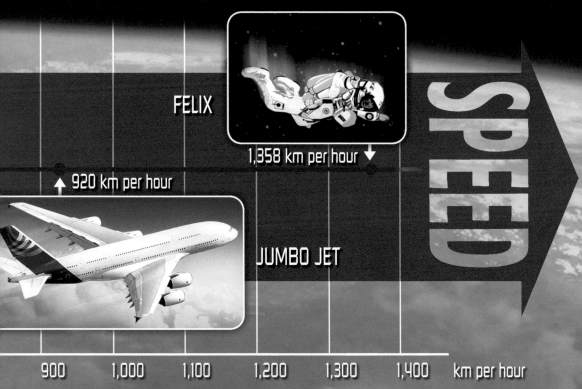

FELIX

1,358 km per hour

920 km per hour

JUMBO JET

SPEED

| 900 | 1,000 | 1,100 | 1,200 | 1,300 | 1,400 | km per hour |

Felix needed a specially designed pod to take him to the jump point on the edge of space. At that height, there isn't enough oxygen in the air to breathe, so the pod was designed to be **airtight**. It would provide him with oxygen to breathe on his long journey upwards.

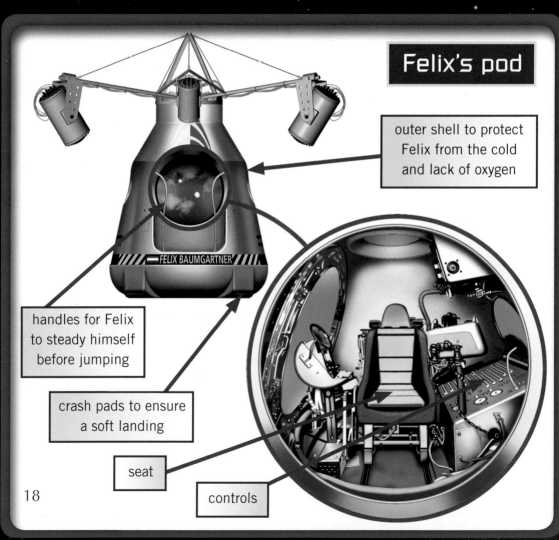

Felix's pod

outer shell to protect Felix from the cold and lack of oxygen

handles for Felix to steady himself before jumping

crash pads to ensure a soft landing

seat

controls

FELIX BAUMGARTNER

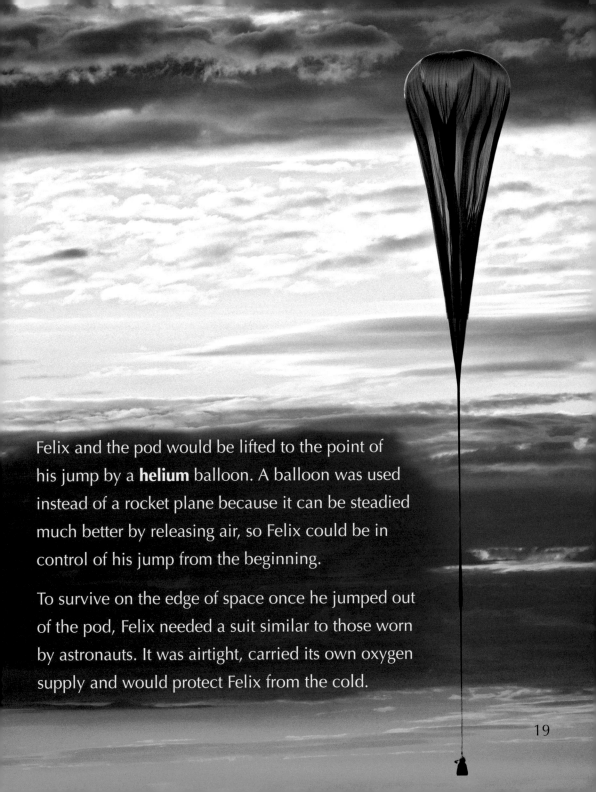

Felix and the pod would be lifted to the point of his jump by a **helium** balloon. A balloon was used instead of a rocket plane because it can be steadied much better by releasing air, so Felix could be in control of his jump from the beginning.

To survive on the edge of space once he jumped out of the pod, Felix needed a suit similar to those worn by astronauts. It was airtight, carried its own oxygen supply and would protect Felix from the cold.

19

Felix's preparation

For Felix to succeed, he needed to be at the peak of his mental and physical fitness. He would have to be alert and focused, and he would need all his strength to move in the pressure suit. He spent lots of time in the gym. Doctors monitored his health to ensure he was fit enough for the jump.

He practised floating in a wind tunnel to help him prepare for free falling. He even did bungee jumps in the suit to prepare for stepping off the pod. Colonel Joe Kittinger was there to advise Felix throughout his training.

Large fans in the bottom of the wind tunnel create a strong wind going upward. The wind lifts people into the air so they can practise free falling in a safe place.

Before the jump, it was important for Felix to get used to his
pressure suit. At first he felt very uncomfortable because
the enclosed suit was difficult to move in.

He also spent a lot of time in the pod getting used to
the cramped conditions.

Felix would be on his own during his jump. But in **Mission Control**, Colonel Joe Kittinger and many doctors, scientists and engineers were stationed on the ground to help.

The scientists and engineers at Mission Control ensured that Felix's equipment was working properly before the mission began. They would also monitor his progress from lift off to landing.

As well as helping and advising Felix before the jump, Colonel Joe Kittinger played an important part during the mission. It was Joe's responsibility to maintain contact with Felix throughout the entire mission. If Felix got into trouble, Joe would know what to do and be able to help.

The space jump

Before the space jump, Felix completed two test jumps in New Mexico to check the balloon, pod, pressure suit and parachute system were working properly. The first test jump was from 22 kilometres, 17 kilometres lower than the planned jump, and the second was from 30 kilometres, 9 kilometres lower. Both jumps were successful. Felix was ready.

Felix entering the pod before the space jump

On 14 October 2012, Felix prepared to attempt the highest ever skydive, at 39 kilometres – from the edge of space.

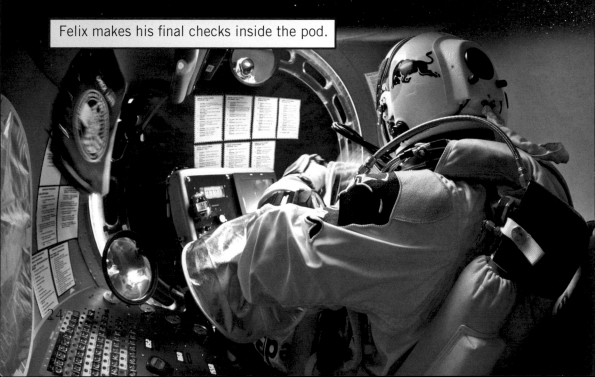

Felix makes his final checks inside the pod.

At 9:28 a.m., at the Roswell International Air Center in New Mexico, the helium-filled balloon was released and floated off the ground. Felix sat in the pod underneath.

For two and a half hours, the balloon, pod and Felix rose higher and higher. All the while, Colonel Joe Kittinger was talking Felix through every step.

At 39 kilometres, the balloon had gone as high as the helium could take it and Felix stopped going any higher.

At 12:06 p.m., Felix looked down and jumped.

Felix was free falling and gaining speed from the moment he left the pod.

After 42 seconds he reached his maximum speed – 1,358 kilometres per hour. He was falling faster than the speed of sound.

But Felix lost control of his fall and began to spin. He was spinning quickly for about 30 seconds but his years of skydiving experience allowed him to regain control.

After four minutes, 20 seconds of free fall, Felix released his parachute at a height of 2,500 metres. He touched down in the desert in New Mexico nine minutes after jumping from the pod. Felix's pod returned to the ground using its own parachute.

Felix's world records

Felix broke three official world records during the space jump.

1 Highest speed without a vehicle: **1,358 kilometres per hour**

2 Highest skydive: **39 kilometres**

3 Furthest free fall without a vehicle: **36 kilometres**

Felix's team learnt many things. The scientists and engineers gathered information to help make flight equipment safer, and the medical experts found out how heights and speeds affect the human body.

During his fall, Felix's heart reached 185 beats per minute. The average rate for a man is 70 beats per minute. The space jump proved that with the right equipment, team and training a human can survive **accelerating** to speeds beyond the speed of sound. Felix had succeeded. He had broken the record for the highest skydive. He had made history.

Glossary

accelerating — making something go faster

airtight — not allowing air to move in or out

atmosphere — gases surrounding the earth

consciousness — being awake and aware

free falls — the first stage of a parachute jump, before the parachute opens

helium — a gas used to fill balloons – it is lighter than air

Mission Control — the people who direct an aircraft and its crew from lift off to landing

promoted — supported and encouraged an organisation

special forces — highly trained military forces who work on difficult missions

29

Majlis al Jinn cave base jump
121 metres deep

Taipei 101 skydive
509 metres

Christ the Redeemer base jump
29 metres

**English Channel
skydive**
9.8 kilometres

space jump
39 kilometres

Ideas for reading

Written by Gillian Howell
Primary Literacy Consultant

Learning objectives: *(word reading objectives correspond with Lime band; all other objectives correspond with Diamond band)* read aloud books closely matched to their improving phonic knowledge, sounding out unfamiliar words accurately, automatically and without undue hesitation; reading books that are structured in different ways and reading for a range of purposes; summarising the main ideas drawn from more than one paragraph, identifying key details that support the main ideas

Curriculum links: Science, Geography

Interest words: mechanic, parachute, courage, equipment, Colonel, scientists, designers, atmosphere, stratosphere, consciousness, pressure, accelerating

Word count: 2,000

Resources: pens, paper, art materials, internet

Getting started

- Read the title and discuss the front cover with the children. Ask them what they think a space jump is and what they can see in the picture.

- Read the blurb together. Ask the children to suggest what personal characteristics they think someone would need to have to be a record-breaking skydiver.

- Ask them to read the contents page and find the glossary. Ask them to read the glossary and definitions of terms to familiarise themselves with the words before reading.

Reading and responding

- Ask the children to read the book and make notes on what previous experiences Felix had of extreme sports and what preparation he undertook before the space jump.

- Listen to the children as they read, and occasionally ask them to describe any extra information they can glean from the photos.